# AN ILLUSTRATED HISTORY OF

# Trucks

## and Buses

Gillian Stuart.

# AN ILLUSTRATED HISTORY OF

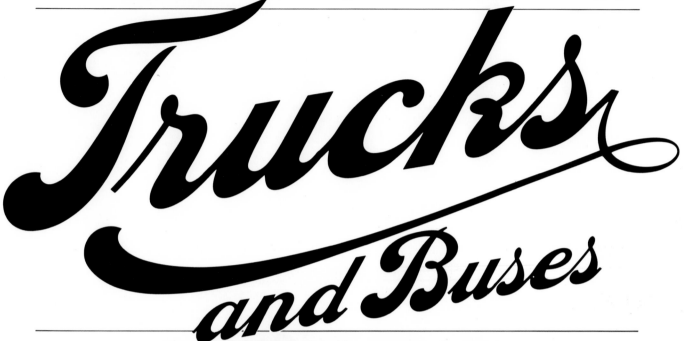

# Trucks
## and Buses

## BY DENIS MILLER

NEW
BURLINGTON
BOOKS

A QUARTO BOOK

Published in the United Kingdom 1982 by New Burlington
Books Ltd, London W1

© 1982 Quarto Limited

ISBN 0 906286 15 8

Typeset by Everbest Printing Company Ltd., Hong Kong
Colour separations by Rodney Howe, England
Printed in Hong Kong by Lee Fung-Asco Printers Ltd

This book was designed and produced by
Quarto Publishing Limited, 32 Kingly Court,
London W1


Designers: Nick Clark
Andrew Fenton


Design Assistant: Tony Paine
Art Director: Bob Morley
Project Editor: Caroline Schuck
Editors: Victoria Funk
Jane Struthers
Richard Williams

Editorial Director: Jeremy Harwood

*Opposite page:* A heavy-duty Scammell truck on
the road. After the Second World War, the heavy
vehicle industry continued the dramatic expansion
that had been a feature of the war years.

*Endpapers:* Two Autocars, working on the eastern
section of the Lincoln Highway, linking New
York and Omaha, in about 1919. Road and
truck development went hand-in-hand during
this period.

# Contents

# An idea is born

THE MAN generally credited with developing the world's first practical self-propelled vehicle in 1769 is Captain Nicolas Joseph Cugnot, of the Artillerie Française, although there were numerous other experiments prior to this time. The earliest recorded attempt was made by the German, Johann Hautach, who, in the sixteenth century, constructed a horseless carriage apparently propelled by a system of coiled springs. One century later, two Englishmen, Ramsay and Wildgoose, patented another design. Both types were purely experimental, however, and it is unlikely that they ever ran on a public highway.

Cugnot worked hard, first building a model steam carriage to illustrate his ideas. The French government was favourably impressed and ordered him to construct a full-size model, which was demonstrated in front of the French Minister of War. Although the demonstration proved that the design was not quite as reliable as it could have been, a second machine was ordered with a 4½-ton payload capable of hauling field artillery on level ground at a speed of 6km/h. In spite of being crude and clumsy, this vehicle was a comparative success.

In 1784, while working for the Cornish steam engine manufacturers Boulton and Watt, William Murdock, a young Scottish mechanic, built his first steam carriage, but this was not particularly successful, and again appears never to have run on the public highway. Meanwhile, Oliver Evans, a Welsh inventor living in the United States, was investigating the possibility of applying steam power to a road-going carriage, and in 1787 was granted the exclusive right to develop such a machine in the State of Maryland. No actual wagon appears to have materialized, although in 1804 he fitted wheels to a 20-ton steam dredger and drove it under its own power to the River Schuylkill, along which he sailed to Delaware. This was undoubtedly the world's first self-propelled amphibious vehicle, and Evans's ideas also formed the first US patent for a self-propelled steam road vehicle in 1789. A year later, Charles Dalley, of Amiens, France, constructed a rela-

*Above* The world's oldest surviving self-propelled vehicle is Cugnot's 1770 artillery tractor. *Left* In 1833 Dr F. Church designed a very ornate machine, which even had springs supporting the simple front wheel. *Opposite left* One year after the success of Trevithick's first self-propelled steam carriage in 1801, he constructed a new model *Opposite top right* This replica of William Murdock's steam vehicle of 1784 shows steam propulsion at its simplest. *Opposite bottom right* Goldsworthy steam carriages were reminiscent of the stage coach, this example was used on Sir Charles Dance's Gloucester-Cheltenham run.

tively successful steam carriage, while in America both Apollo Kinsley of Hartford, Connecticut, and Nathan Read, of Eden, Massachusetts, developed vehicles of this type.

In the United Kingdom, Richard Trevithick, who already held the distinction of building the world's first steam railway locomotive, constructed the world's first self-propelled steam carriage to run successfully on public roads. It appeared in 1801. One year later Trevithick's second steam carriage was completed, but lack of finance curtailed further development. It was the lack of funds which also hampered other early experiments in the field, particularly in the United Kingdom, where many financiers already had a vested interest in other forms of transport, such as canals and railways, and were unlikely to show

much enthusiasm for a competitive activity. It may well have been this lack of financial backing that led to an economy of design which precipitated serious, and often fatal, accidents involving early self-propelled vehicles such as boiler explosions, and steering and brake failures, none of which did anything to instil enthusiasm for this new mode of transport.

Goldsworthy Gurney was quick to realize that safety had to come first if the public was to have any confidence in mechanical road transport, and by 1827, following experiments with three alternative types of boiler, he had constructed his first steam coach. Having perfected a "safe" boiler, he then looked for other improvements, deciding to use coke, which was smokeless, for fuel, rather than coal. Within a year he had perfected his de-

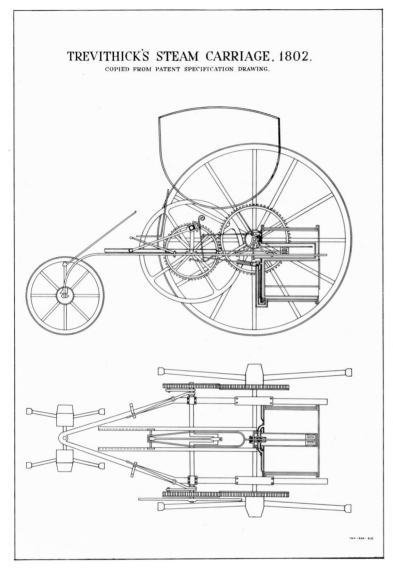

TREVITHICK'S STEAM CARRIAGE, 1802.
COPIED FROM PATENT SPECIFICATION DRAWING.

sign with one machine completing a 135-km run between Melksham, Wilts, and Cranford, Middx, in just ten hours. Sir Charles Dance was a Gurney customer who improved the specification still further and, in 1831, inaugurated a service which ran four times a day along a 14-km route between Gloucester and Cheltenham at an average speed, including stops, of 16 to 19km/h. Other routes followed, but both official and unofficial opposition forced him to close down.

One of the most successful of all United Kingdom steam carriage builders was Walter Hancock, who built his first machine in 1827. Again, safety was of prime consideration, and the first Hancock coach embodied a chain transmission and tight metal boiler joints to withstand high pressures. In 1828 the French engineer

Onesiphore Pecqueur designed and patented a 4-ton steam truck, but construction is not recorded.

Opposition to steam-powered road vehicles in the United Kingdom grew rapidly, with many influential people being against the project. As a result, in 1831 a series of prohibitive bills were passed by the British government to discourage the development of steam vehicles.

The world's first automotive publication, *The Journal of Elemental Locomotion*, was founded by Alexander Gordon in 1832. Sir Goldsworthy Gurney did much to reverse the government's attitude and an attempt was made to form the United Kingdom's first public passenger transport company. This was the London, Holyhead & Liverpool Steam Coach & Road Co, with a capital of £350,000.

Although it failed, at least the company showed the country's growing awareness of the commercial possibilities of mechanical road transport.

As a result of these moves by the government, the development of steam road propulsion stagnated for thirty years, during which time many pioneers turned to the railways and steam shipping.

While the development of self-propelled road vehicles had been largely halted, there were numerous developments on the agricultural front, where portable steam engines, previously hauled by horses, were now being converted to self-propulsion.

By the 1850s, some of the more intrepid inventors were again looking at road vehicles and, despite their being illegal in the United Kingdom, demonstrations frequently took place on

the public highways. This unfortunately led to the crippling Locomotive Acts of 1861 and 1865, and to the Highways & Locomotives (Amendment) Act of 1878. Thus, as Continental and American inventors raced ahead, so their British counterparts were left behind.

While this was taking place in the United Kingdom, in France, Joseph Ravel had taken out a patent in 1868 for "a steam generator heated by mineral oils supplied to steam locomotives on ordinary roads and to all industrial purposes", which was later developed into a petroleum-fuelled steamer. An Englishman, Joseph Wilkinson, is also said to have developed such a system and J H Knight, of Farnham, Surrey, had built a 1½-ton steam carriage. Another French development was the gas engine invented by Etienne Lenoir in 1860, in which gas was mixed with air and ignited by electricity. This was used in the inventor's first horseless carriage two years later. By 1872 the first engine to use fuel oil rather than gas was patented in the United Kingdom by George Brayton, and three years later what may have been the world's first self-propelled load-carrier was created – a 4-ton steam wagon constructed by Brown & May, of Devizes, Wilts. Unfortunately, Brayton's idea was developed into designs for a complete vehicle by George Baldwin Selden, Rochester, New York, in 1879 and led ultimately to a US patent being granted in 1895, in which anyone else using an internal-combustion engine in a road vehicle had to pay royalties to Selden. This arrangement held until 1911 and did much to stunt motor industry growth in the United States.

However, the greatest advances were about to be made in Germany, and were to be crucial to the development of heavy trucks and buses.

Karl Benz was the son of an engine driver, and attended an engineering course at the Karlsruhe Polytechnic before joining a local railway locomotive builder. He became fascinated with the theories of Professor Redtenbacher at the Polytechnic, and as a result turned his attention to the development of the internal-combus-

tion engine for road vehicles. Soon Benz had set up his own business, as a manufacturer of stationary gas engines and in 1885, at his Mannheim premises, his first motor car, a 3-wheeler, began to take shape. This was the world's first internal-combustion engined passenger car and set numerous precedents for the future. Drive was transmitted to a countershaft and then by chain and sprocket to the rear wheels, while other features included liquid cooling and an electric ignition system.

Another German pioneer was Gottlieb Daimler, who worked in many parts of Europe before settling in Germany and developing oil engines with Dr Nickolaus August Otto and Eugen Langen. Neither of the latter saw much future in the use of the internal-

combustion engine to provide power for road vehicles, so, in 1882, Daimler resigned and was joined at an experimental workshop in Cannstatt by Wilhelm Maybach, another ex-employee of Otto and Langen. Their first gas engine was a single-cyl air-cooled horizontal unit which was followed, in 1883, by a fully-enclosed design with tube ignition which, by 1885, was being used to power a motorized bicycle. Daimler's first car appeared in 1886. This was a converted horse-drawn carriage powered by a 1½hp single-cyl air-cooled unit with 2-speed transmission via a friction clutch to the rear wheels. An improved model, with differential gear and a 4-speed transmission, appeared in 1889, this having a rear-mounted single-cyl vertical water-cooled engine and all-gear final

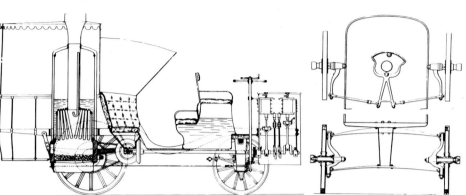

*Opposite top* Richard Dudgeon, of New York, constructed a passenger steam road vehicle in 1850 which ran successfully for nearly ten years. *Opposite bottom* The most successful steam carriage inventor of the period was Walter Hancock who built and operated 'Autopsy', 'Era' and 'Infant'. *Above* Amédée Bollée Snr who constructed this carriage in 1873 was a leading French advocate of steam-propulsion. *Top right* A front-mounted vertical-twin engine was combined with a rear-mounted vertical boiler in this Amédée Bollée design of 1878. *Right* The Grenville steam carriage was built in Britain in 1875 employing a rear-mounted vertical boiler.

drive. Daimler's third attempt incorporated belt transmission and a 'V'-twin engine, and was one of the most important landmarks in the early days of motoring. Simultaneously, Benz was improving his self-propelled 3-wheeler, but it was in 1891 that his first 4-wheeled passenger car was built.

While these ideas were taking shape in Germany, the French were also hard at work. In 1890 Léon Serpollet took a significant step in the development of steam propulsion for road vehicles by inventing the "flash" boiler. Meanwhile, Panhard et Levassor, Paris, which had been appointed an agent for Daimler gas and oil engines, was soon developing in 1891 the world's first "real" passenger car, using a ladder-type chassis frame and full working drawings. Powered by a

'V'-twin Daimler engine mounted vertically at the front, this had a clutch and sliding 3-speed pinion transmission and marked the dawn of the motor car.

The first self-propelled vehicle to be exported from the United States was a steam carriage built by R E Olds which was delivered to the Francis Times Co, Bombay, India. In the United Kingdom, Hornsby & Son developed its first oil engine the following year. The Germans, however, were in the forefront of internal-combustion engine developments, and were now regularly supplying such units to other road vehicle builders throughout the Western world.

For the time being, however, Maurice LeBlant's 1892 steam vans, with Serpollet boilers and 3-cyl engines

with steersman at the front and stoker at the rear, were about the only self-propelled load-carriers in Europe. One was entered in the world's first motor vehicle trial between Paris and Rouen in 1894, but was only marginally successful. Also in 1894, an experimental 5-ton steam wagon was built at Leyland, Lancs, by the young James Sumner, forming the foundations of the world-renowned commercial vehicle manufacturer, Leyland Vehicles.

The first light commercials were also French, derived from Panhard et Levassor and Peugeot passenger car designs and there were also battery-electric types such as those built by Jeantaud and Krieger. The next two years, however, were to see the dawn of the internal-combustion engined commercial vehicle.

# Fire engines

The lure of the fire engine is universal. From small boys to grown men, the sound of the siren stops all in their tracks just as the clanging bell and clattering hooves did at the turn of the century. When originally developed, the fire engine was a means of combating fire but can now handle a multitude of diverse tasks the most important of which is rescue. Thus, a host of special machinery has been designed, often mounted on specially developed reliable chassis capable of high-speed operation. While many truck manufacturers have, from time to time, offered a fire engine chassis, it is the specialist companies such as American LaFrance, Dennis, Merryweather, Seagrave and Ward LaFrance that have become world famous in this field.

1

2

3

7  6

4

5

8

9

10

1 In 1903 Merryweather & Sons Ltd supplied the world's first petrol-engined chemical appliance to the Tottenham Fire Brigade.
2 The Dependable Truck & Tractor Co, Illinois, built this chemical appliance around 1921.
3 As early as 1907, Gobron-Brillié had combined a petrol-engined chassis with a steam-powered pump. 4 The Dennis was the most popular British appliance of the 1920s and 30s. 5 In 1952 the Dennis F8 appliance appeared. It was used as a motor pump. 6 This American LaFrance has an artic aerial ladder truck.
7 Comparatively rare as a fire appliance, this Bedford RMA was fitted with a hydraulic watertower.
8 In 1977 the 6x6 Oshkosh 'M'-Series was launched for special use on airfields.
9 Daimler-Benz offers the 4x4 Unimags with chemical foam equipment for industrial use.
10 The White 'Road Xpeditor 2'.

# The experimental years

HORSELESS CARRIAGE FEVER was now rife throughout Europe, the United States, and the United Kingdom. By the mid-1890s there were many entrepreneurs in road vehicle development, but one man in particular got things underway in the United Kingdom. He was Sir David Salomons who, as a skilled engineer and Mayor of Tunbridge Wells, Kent, organized what was probably the world's first horseless carriage exhibition, on the Tunbridge Wells Agricultural Showground in 1895. Although only five vehicles (including a Daimler-engined Panhard et Levassor motor fire pump and a De Dion-Bouton "steam horse") were present, the event attracted much attention.

One month later, the inaugural meeting of the Self-Propelled Traffic Association (SPTA) was held in London, again organized by Sir David, but with the assistance of Frederick Richard Simms, another motoring pioneer who was a director of Daimler Motoren Gesellschaft. He had been responsible for establishing Daimler products in the United Kingdom and had developed an automatic fuel feed system for carburettors. The idea behind the SPTA was to put pressure on the government to repeal the Highways & Locomotives (Amendment) Act of 1878, in order to clear the way for new developments in the automotive field. A deputation was to meet the President of the Board of Agriculture.

With restrictions still in force, there was little hope for the British motor industry, whereas on the Continent, inventors were moving ahead with revolutionary ideas. Some of these were quickly taken up by manufacturers in other countries. Richard F Stewart, New York, United States, for example, used a 2hp Daimler engine and internal-gear drive in his prototype 1895 wagon.

As a prelude to the repeal of the 1878 Act, the Daimler Motor Co was registered in England early in 1896. Chairman was Harry J Lawson, and other directors included such notables as the Hon Evelyn Ellis, Gottlieb Daimler, William Wright, Henry Sturmey, J H Mace, H E Sherwin

Holt and J S Bradshaw. Frederick Simms was Consulting Engineer and J S Critchley was Works Manager. The new company acquired a disused cotton mill in Coventry and was soon in business as the United Kingdom's first motor manufacturer. Lawson also set up the Great Horseless Carriage Co and organized a petition to the House of Commons requesting that the 1878 Act be repealed.

Another Lawson enterprise was the formation of the Motor Car Club (MCC), which was described as "a society for the protection, encourage-

ment and development of the motor car industry". However, it is more likely that it was set up to serve its founder's own ends. One of the first tasks of the MCC was to put on an exhibition of horseless carriages at London's Imperial Institute, opening to the public in May 1896. Every conceivable type of vehicle was present, including a Peugeot-built Daimler bus. While this event was in progress, a Bill repealing the 1878 Act was in preparation.

One of the first production load-carriers in the United States was a pe-

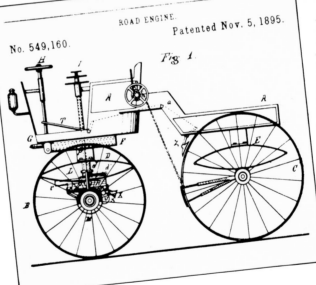

*Far left* John I Thornycroft's 1-ton steam van had front-wheel drive and near wheel steer layout. *Left and above* Selden's steam vehicle which was constructed in the 1870s. In spite of this, it was not patented until 1895 and the patent was worded in such a way that it held back US motor industry development until 1911.

trol-engined wagon entered by the Langert Co, Philadelphia, Pennsylvania, in the 1896 Cosmopolitan Race from New York to Irvington-on-the-Hudson and back. At the same time, a horse-drawn van was converted into a steam wagon by the Cruickshank Engineering Works, Providence, Rhode Island; Charles Woods, Chicago, was alleged to have built the first practical battery-electric commercial; and C S Fairfield, Portland, Oregon, built a kerosene-engined passenger model. In Germany, Daimler Motoren Gesellschaft had built the first purpose-

built Daimler truck – a 2-tonner which, like the company's passenger cars, had the driver at the front and engine at the rear.

The 1878 Act was withdrawn with the introduction of the Locomotives on Highways Act in 1896. This stipulated the speeds at which vehicles could travel. This also stipulated that motor vehicles weighing up to 1½ tons unladen could now travel at up to 18km/h, those weighing between 1½ and 2 tons could travel at up to 12km/h and any vehicle exceeding 2 tons was restricted to 7km/h.

The first commercial load-carrying vehicle in the United Kingdom was a 1-ton steam van with front-wheel drive and rear-wheel steering built by John Isaac Thornycroft, Chiswick, West London. Powered by a Strickland vertical twin marine engine, this was shown at the 1896 Crystal Palace Motor Show organized by Sir David Salomons. It was quickly followed by a 1½-ton steamer built by the Lancashire Steam Motor Co, successor to James Sumner's small business in Leyland, Lancs. In Germany, meanwhile, the Daimler internal-combustion en-

*Above* By 1898 German Daimler trucks had adapted a front-engined layout and they had a tube radiator and pinion drive.
*Right* Completed in 1898, just in time for the Liverpool Heavy Vehicle Trials, this Thornycroft was the world's first artic steam lorry.

gined truck range was being expanded to include models from 1½ to 5 tons capacity with power outputs of up to 10hp.

## Petrol, diesel or steam?

ALTHOUGH REGARDED as a modern means of propulsion, the pioneer work of the diesel was undertaken at the turn of the century, when "heavy" loads were moved by steam. The 1½-ton steam wagon built by the Lancashire Steam Motor Co in 1896 won a Silver Medal at the Royal Agricultural Society's Manchester Trials in 1897. Later that year, the first petrol-engined commercial to be sold in the United Kingdom was a Daimler. At about the same time, MAN of Germany announced the world's first heavy oil engine, and before the end of the year, Daimler adopted a front-engined layout for all commercial models, with the driver positioned on top to provide greater load-carrying area than bonneted types of the same wheelbase. This layout was also used by other manufacturers in the years leading up to 1900, although Daimler himself settled on the bonneted style in 1899, following driver complaints of excessive vibration and difficulty in reaching the vehicle's lofty perch.

In 1898 the American inventor Alexander Winton introduced the first United States petrol-engined load-carrier built in any quantity. A L Riker perfected his design for a series of heavy battery-electric commercials, exemplified by a 1315-kg payload vehicle propelled by batteries weighing 45,359kg, which he exhibited at Madison Square Gardens. It was in the United States that the battery-electric commercial was to have its greatest following during these formative years.

In Germany, Daimler had started to use Bosch magneto ignitions, developed jointly by Robert Bosch and Frederick Simms, which began to woo customers away from steam propulsion. This movement did not, how-

*Left* One of London's first motor-buses was a vulgar-looking Daimler that ran between Oxford Circus and South Kensington. *Below left* Built in 1902, this 3-ton Thornycroft steamer had a vertical water-tube boiler and a compound "undertype" engine. *Below* This steam-powered mail van was shipped to Ceylon in 1901. It was the Lancashire Steam Motor Co's first export order.

# THORNYCROFT

ever, apply to the American market, where oil was plentiful and steam had never figured greatly.

Prompted by the repeal of the 1878 Act, the Liverpool Branch of the Self-Propelled Traffic Association, by then affiliated to the Automobile Club of Great Britain and Ireland, organized the first of a series of heavy vehicle trials in 1898, the second taking place in 1899 and the third in 1901. These were held at the instigation of the Liverpool Branch's Honorary Secretary, Mr E Shrapnell-Smith, a great enthusiast for mechanical commercial transport, who succeeded in his wish of encouraging the manufacture of such vehicles.

By 1899 Thornycroft's steam wagons were becoming popular as tippers and refuse collectors, as well as seeing active service in the Boer War. The same company had also completed work on the world's first steam-powered articulated lorry. Generally, however, there was no standard mode of propulsion, the choice ranging through steam, petrol, kerosene and electricity.

The heavy oil or diesel engine should not be forgotten, as eventually it would become almost universally accepted for use in heavy commercials. Despite Rudolf Diesel's pioneering work in Germany (his main achievement being the development

of an automatic ignition system using compressed air) it was two Englishmen, Priestman and Ackroyd Stuart, who developed the heavy oil engine as we know it today. Priestman adopted a system whereby fuel was injected into a cylinder-held pocket of air at maximum pressure and he had the world's first oil-engined lorry on the road by 1897. Meanwhile, Ackroyd Stuart developed the hot bulb ignition system, which replaced the external method used by Priestman and others.

Steam vehicles excepted, commercial load-carrying development paralleled that of the passenger car, which was more noticeable in the lighter designs. Steamers were especially popular in the United Kingdom, where plentiful supplies of comparatively cheap coal and coke were readily available. Such machines were normally of "undertype" layout, with engine slung beneath the chassis frame and a vertical boiler located ahead of, or behind, the driver, thereby providing maximum load space. Engine accessibility was poor, and boilers were often inefficient, but the solutions to these problems were to be found in the United Kingdom by 1901.

The last year of the nineteenth century saw some bus operators experimenting with self-propelled vehicles, but it was still to be some time before these ousted the ever-faithful horse. From 1900 onwards, however, the development of the self-propelled commercial load-carrier was to become even more fascinating than that of the passenger motor car.

## The truck revolution

THE COMMERCIAL VEHICLE was by no means a European idea, because it was at this time that the United States began vehicle trials, thereby increasing the interest in such vehicles in the country.

With the turn of the century, the internal-combustion engine had yet to prove itself. Unreliability continued to be a major obstacle to commercial acceptance and business people generally regarded it as more for the mad motoring public than as being reliable for goods delivery. Horse-drawn or steam vehicles were accepted as the ideal choice for work of this nature. In an attempt to counteract this attitude and establish the internal-combustion engined vehicle in business circles, the British Automobile Club set up the Motor Van, Wagon & Omnibus Users' Association, which subsequently provided much of the impetus required.

By 1900 Daimler had built the world's first charabanc, and the German Army was undertaking field trials with a Daimler lorry. In 1901 the world's first mechanical street sweeper was built by the American, John Collins, of Connecticut, and an American subsidiary of the German

*Top* Leyland Motors Ltd received one of the first Royal Warrants granted to a British Motor manufacturer for a shooting van which they built in 1910 for King George V. The warrant is shown above the van together with the Leyland logo. *Above* Affectionately known as "The Pig", the first petrol-engined Leyland was a 1½-ton truck. *Left* While petrol-engined vehicles were now dealing with the lighter loads, a 6 ton steamer, such as this Leyland, was used for larger consignments.

*Right* The Manhattan sight-seeing bus of 1904 was one of the earliest production vehicles built in the United States by the Mack brothers. *Above* By 1910 Reliant trucks were reaching the end of the line as a marque in their own right, having already been taken over by General Motors. *Below* Early Daimler ideas were now being reflected in other marques such as this three ton Bussing made in 1902.

Daimler organization set up what is believed to have been the world's first truck service and tow-in scheme. On the steam front, the British firm of Fodens Ltd introduced the efficient loco-type horizontal boiler and "over-type" engine on a new wagon, which was quickly copied, despite the fact that it occupied more load space. In 1902 the first petrol-engined Thornycroft commercial appeared, a 2-ton lorry, relying upon experience gained from the manufacture of internal-combustion engined passenger cars. This company did not forsake its steam wagons, and later developed a demountable body system for its municipal steamers. In 1904, the John S Muir Syndicate announced a steam-powered sweeper/sprinkler which was another first in the municipal field.

America's first truck contest was organized in May 1903 by the newly formed Automobile Club of America, using a two-stage course starting from the club's headquarters in New York's Fifth Avenue. It was a two-day event, with entries divided into two classes, delivery wagons and heavy trucks, the former having to complete 64km a day and the latter 48km. All entries had to be fully laden, the winners on both days being a Knox-Waterless and a Herschmann steamer. As in the United Kingdom, this event encouraged the growth of vehicle manufacture. A specialist journal, *The Horseless Age,* commented that delivery wagons had now "arrived".

On the passenger vehicle scene, London witnessed numerous experiments with mechanically-propelled vehicles of this type, many being steam-powered and a frightening experience to the many horse-drawn vehicles still in operation. The first fleet of self-propelled buses to be used appears to have been that of the London General Omnibus Co, which had a number of vehicles in service by 1904. Among early experiments were those of the London Road Car Co, which introduced a few Maudslay buses as early as 1902. The Maudslay Motor Co Ltd, Coventry, was a pioneer in the development of the British commercial vehicle industry, using many advanced features in its designs.

One such was the single-piece axle; another was removable inspection plates in the engine crankcase to facilitate big-end inspection and the removal of damaged connecting rods or pistons.

By this time, United Kingdom speed restrictions had been relaxed and the Lancashire Steam Motor Co announced its first internal-combustion engined commercial – a 1½-ton model affectionately known as "The Pig". A new type of passenger vehicle which became popular at this time was the charabanc, with each row of seats being slightly higher than the one in front, to provide all passengers with a good view of the road ahead. Until the passenger car became a viable proposition for the working classes, the charabanc took pride of place in many fleets, particularly those based in coastal and tourist areas.

On the other side of the Atlantic, another commercial vehicle test was held in New York in April 1904, to encourage more firms to build such vehicles. Many were of driver-over-engine layout, as in the case of the first Daimlers, and by the end of 1904 the first power-assisted steering system had been developed. A year later petrol-engined buses ran for the first time on New York's fashionable Fifth Avenue.

For city deliveries, the heavy battery-electric wagon was coming into its own but was restricted to a particular operating base, where its batteries could be re-charged. The battery-electric had both advantages and disadvantages. One advantage was that it was comparatively easy to maintain, while, on the negative side, the batteries were exceptionally heavy – until Thomas Edison discovered the iron-nickel-alkaline battery in 1908. Such machines were also ponderously slow, often necessitating the use of two or even four traction motors, usually mounted in the vehicle's wheels.

In the United Kingdom, in March 1905, the first edition of *Commercial Motor* appeared (later to become one of the most important heavy automotive journals in the world) with E Shrapnell-Smith as Editor, joined three months later by *Motor Traction*.

The trade paper 'The Commercial Motor' first came out on 16 March, 1905. It was priced at one penny and included advertisements for truck parts as well as for trucks.

*Top left* The VCPL bus was unique in having two engines slung beneath the vehicle. Each of these engines supplied current to an electric motor at each rear wheel. *Next row extreme left* C A Tilt's first truck, a 1½-ton Diamond T which he built in 1911. He quickly introduced other models with capacities up to 5 tons. *Left* This 5-ton "overtype" wagon was a rarity, built by "undertype" pioneer Alley and McLellon Ltd. *Below and bottom* While Adolph Saurer AG, Switzerland was exporting ambulances to Russia, a plant was being set up in the USA and a US-built 4-tonner was sent on a transcontinental publicity run. The Saurer logo is shown to the right of the picture.

Meanwhile, in Lavender Hill, South London, Commercial Motors Ltd had been set up to pursue the commercial possibilities of the Linley pre-select gearbox. A 4-ton iron-wheeled lorry called the CC was constructed, which was to become the Commer. The development of the new transmission systems occupied a great deal of thought at this time. Some, such as Panhard, used a sliding-tooth system, and others, such as DeDion, left the gears in mesh, with gear-changing effected by the use of expanding friction clutches. There were also planetary or constant-mesh systems, and the German inventor, Dr H Föttinger, even developed an automatic system.

The first American motor truck show was held in Chicago in 1907, and the world's first steam vacuum cesspool emptier, developed by Merryweather & Sons Ltd, appeared in 1908. The latter made the self-propelled vehicle more important than it had been in local authorities. The Chicago event attracted attention on both sides of the Atlantic, due to the publicity surrounding a 489-km test run accomplished by a 3-ton petrol-engined Reliance in less than four days. A 1609-km commercial vehicle trial for 19 petrol-engined 3-tonners and 10 petrol- and steam-powered 5-tonners was organized by the Automobile Club in 1907. The first British Commercial Motor Show was held at Olympia, London, in the same year, under the jurisdiction of the Society of Motor Manufacturers & Traders. These events finally set the commercial vehicle on the map.

Some manufacturers were now turning from steam to petrol, although few completely abandoned the former. Thus, the Lancashire Steam Motor Co became Leyland Motors Ltd, and two petrol-engined lorries were the first internal-combustion engined Thornycrofts to receive a War Office diploma. The Swiss Saurer company was now converting 4-cyl Safir petrol engines into diesel units, and developed an engine brake which compressed air inside the engine, converting it into a retarder. This same company was soon exporting petrol-engined trucks worldwide. Other sig-

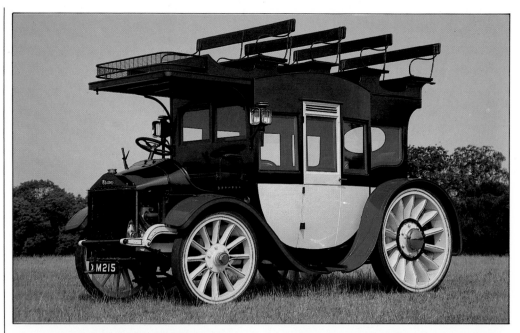

nificant advances included the first closed-top double-deck bus and trolleybus experiments were held in North London.

Elsewhere, the first production articulated lorry was seen, namely the unusual 3-wheeled Knox, built in Springfield, Massachusetts, United States. A major development of 1909 was Sven Winquist's ball-race system for commercial vehicle wheels, successfully tested in a new Scania truck between Malmo and Stockholm in Sweden.

The London General Omnibus Co Ltd (LGOC) had meanwhile been busy acquiring various independent operators, but was finding its motley collection of self-propelled buses

none too reliable. Accordingly, the Associated Equipment Co, which was responsible for the LGOC's maintenance facilities, began constructing its own vehicles in Walthamstow. The first was the AEC 'X'-Type, followed before the end of 1910 by the most advanced open-top double-decker seen so far – the famous 'B'-Type with ultra-lightweight chassis and body, conforming to police regulations limiting the gross weight to 3½ tons. Instead of the more popular channel-steel frame, the 'B'-Type was of ash wood with nickel-steel flitch plates, apparently used to counteract vibration.

Another model which was gaining popularity was the Tilling-Stevens pe-

*Top left* The 24-seat Thames coach, resembling a motorized stage coach, was another oddity of the pre-World War II days. *Far left top* George A Brockway's first truck was this bonneted high-wheeler, a design typical of many US manufacturers of the period. *Far left bottom* The Reo 'Democrat' wagon introduced in 1911 by R E Old's Reo Motor Car Co was another vehicle which followed the high-wheeler principle. *Left* The LGOC's 'B'-Type double decker revolutionized London's public transport system and during the war it provided transport to the Front. *Right* Despite the general acceptance of a bonneted layout, there were still a few strange designs around in 1911 when this French Berliet 'CAT'-Type was built.

trol-electric, which eliminated gear-changing, making a driver's transition from horse to internal-combustion driving that much easier. Another vehicle which used a similar system was the KPL, built by the Daimler Motor Co Ltd, Coventry. This was even more revolutionary, being of integral construction with two Knight sleeve-valve petrol engines coupled to two traction motors which, in turn, were connected to each rear wheel. Four-wheel brakes were another unusual feature.

Following the country's first War Department vehicle trials, Britain's first "subsidy" scheme was devised, whereby an operator buying a lorry conforming to a particular specifica-tion was entitled to an annual subsidy of £110, provided the vehicle was available to the military authorities, within 72 hours, in an emergency. By 1911 both Leeds and Bradford were running the first British trolleybus fleets. The "subsidy" scheme did much to establish conformity amongst British vehicle manufacturers.

The world's first tiltcab truck was the American-built Pope-Hartford of 1912, and in 1913 an even more unusual design, the 2/3-ton Austin twin-shaft lorry, was announced. The inauguration of the world's first true motor truck assembly line at the Ford Motor Co plant, Dearborn, Michigan, took place in 1914, resulting in the United States becoming a world lead-er in truck production. Meanwhile, Sydney Guy, formerly of Sunbeam, unveiled his first commercial, a 1½-ton design with one of the first over-drive transmissions, a road speed governor and, even rarer, detachable overhead valves.

By the time World War I broke out, there had been many other advances in the commercial vehicle field. Steam wagons, for example, were now shod with solid rubber tyres instead of the noisy steel units fitted to earlier models, and internal-combustion engined commercials were rapidly replacing the horse. New bus services were being established in most countries and, because of the competitiveness of operators, advances were rapid.

# Buses

Road passenger transport in the early 1900s was undertaken by goods chassis fitted with passenger-carrying bodies. Bus services were maintained by single- and double-deckers, the latter open-topped, with very high floor levels and it was not unusual for some operators to run a single chassis with two bodies – one for goods, the other for passengers. By the 1920s this attitude was changing and lower-loading passenger chassis were appearing. Greater comfort came about through the introduction of pneumatic tyres, covering in top decks and general weather-proofing of bus bodies, while developments of the 1930s brought about greater carrying capacities through the use of multi axles. Chassisless and even articulated types now prevail.

The bus is the workhorse of the road passenger transport industry and the coach is its somewhat upstage sister, with more luxurious accommodation and often capable of higher speeds. The first true coaches were the toastracks and charabancs of the pre World War I era. These were invariably trucks during the week but rebodied at weekends to take parties of trippers to the coast. Many firms up to the 1950s built both buses and coaches, some have since specialised in one or the other and certain European manufacturers are now renowned for their coach models.

1 The earliest motorbuses followed German designs, this open-topped bus, of c.1914, was a British-built Daimler. 2 A Tilling-Stevens with petrol-electric transmission. 3 Glasgow Corporation took delivery of its first batch of BUT single-deck trolleybuses around 1953. These were unique to Glasgow and had 36-seat centre-entrance standee bodies. 4 LGOC brought in their S-Type, a 54-seat double decker bus which they launched on London. 5 This Bristol K5G was originally delivered to the Hants and Dorset Motor Services Ltd in 1940. In 1954 it was rebodied and used as an open-topper sea front bus. 6 These 1948 MCI 'Courier' single-deckers lined up at Windsor, Ontario, were typical of North American and Canadian passenger models of the late 1940s and early '50s. 7 The first two Birmingham-built Metrobuses to be used in London ran on the number 16 route between Cricklewood Garage and Victoria. 8 The most common Swiss postal coach was the Saurer. For many years the postal coach was unique to Switzerland but it is now familiar in a number of countries. 9 This Leyland 'Tiger Cub' operated by Watt Bros City Coast Buses, Queensland, Australia is similar to the MCI Courier.

# The great war

AN IMMEDIATE DEMAND for mechanical military transport following the declaration of war in Europe was partly solved by a considerable influx of well-engineered cross-country trucks from the United States. Those countries that had prepared in advance by introducing "subsidy" schemes soon found they were in a far superior position to those that had not. Despite this, problems abounded.

Steam-powered vehicles such as traction engines had been used on a small scale in earlier situations, but the internal-combustion engined truck had never been used in war conditions, and weaknesses in design were soon apparent. These included insufficient power, lack of ground clearance, and poor protection of mechanical units from the ravages of water and mud, for which the Flanders battlefields were soon renowned. There was, however, another major problem that few had foreseen. Both sides in the conflict used many components supplied by firms on the opposing side: German-manufactured Bosch magnetos were used almost exclusively by the Allies, while German forces relied largely upon British- and French-manufactured Dunlop and Michelin tyres. Luckily, the Bosch magneto had been developed jointly by Robert Bosch and the American Frederick Simms, and German supplies were replaced by magnetos from the Simms Magneto Co factory, Watsersing, New Jersey.

At this stage it is worth looking in depth at some of the "subsidy" schemes operating at the time. The instigators of this idea were the Germans who, in the years prior to 1914, had been building up their military reserves. The German scheme is understood to have applied to any truck which an operator was prepared to release to the military upon mobilization. The operator received an initial grant of £150 towards the purchase of the vehicle, followed by a subsidy of £60 for each of the next four years. By the time war was declared, some 825 "subsidy" trucks had been released to the German Armed Forces.

A similar scheme was organized by the French government, and the British system, in which there were two classes of load-carrying vehicle – a 1½-tonner and a 3-tonner – brought about the first signs of standardization in the

*Above* Leyland's 'RAF'-Type 3-tonner was one of the best known British 'subsidy' types. *Right* After the war many of these vehicles were resold onto the civilian market, like this Chivers' van.

*Left* Many "Tommies", such as these members of the 2nd Battalion Royal Warwickshire Regiment, made their last journeys in London's 'B'-Type buses. *Below* Many British industries could not spare their lorries; this 1915 Fiat 18BL was one of many similar types that remained on the Home Front. *Below centre* Even a 1-ton Studebaker found itself involved in hostilities. Its headlamps were masked so as to make it less of an obvious target. *Bottom* Many vehicles were adapted for military use including this Swiss Saurer 5-tonner.

commercial vehicle industry. The British government offered the purchaser of an approved vehicle a subsidy. However, the vehicle had to be handed over to the authorities within 72 hours of mobilization.

One of the most advanced British "subsidy" types was the 3½-ton Dennis 'A'-Type, although the 'L' or 'RAF'-Type Leyland was certainly the best known. The Dennis had considerable influence on British truck design after the war, its most striking feature being a rear axle with removable upper casing containing the worm shaft, worm wheel, differential and bearings, thus enabling the entire final-drive mechanism to be inspected or replaced without disturbing either the chassis or the wheels. Leyland Motors, on the other hand, built both a 1½-tonner and the 3-ton 'RAF'-Type, while Albion supplied 6000 "subsidy" vehicles, and the Associated Equipment Co Ltd over 10,000. Many of their London General Omni-bus Co 'B'-Type open-top double-deck buses were also commandeered and ordered to the Front. The standardization of models and components required by the British "subsidy" scheme enabled so-called cannibalization to take place to keep transport moving, whereas the adoption of any suitable vehicle by the French and German forces gave no such advantage.

As the war progressed, so British forces began to take delivery of new American-built trucks designed specifically for arduous work. Amongst these was the Mack 'AC', nicknamed the "Bulldog" because of its snub nose and rugged construction. Ultimately, this became so well-known by its nickname that the bulldog was adopted as the Mack logo, which it remains to this day. Some American manufacturers, such as General Motors, were now concentrating almost exclusively on the construction of military vehicles, while certain European manufacturers,

*Below* In 1915 a new series of Internationals were launched. These introduced the 'coal-scuttle' bonnet to the US market. The radiator was carried behind the engine. *Below centre* Large numbers of US-built Peerless 5-tonners were also shipped to Europe. *Bottom left* With increasing competition between manufacturers, publicity stunts such as the GMC milk run from Seattle to New York, became all the rage. *Bottom right* This 1-ton 4x4 built in 1917 by the Wisconsin Duplex Auto Co was the ancestor of the modern Oshkosh range.

*Left* The Mack 'Bulldog', which was a chain-drive model, saw war service in Europe. Its name was apparently coined by British troops who thought that the pugnacious styling of the steel hood resembled a bulldog. The bulldog was quickly adopted as the company symbol. *Below* This early drawbar model of the 'Bulldog' series was produced in America. Even today examples of it can be found in various parts of the world.

such as MAN, Magirus in Germany or Société d'Outillage Mécanique et d'Usinage d'Artilleries (Somua) in France, were building their first trucks in an attempt to turn the tide. Indeed, Somua was established for the sole purpose of building army trucks.

Throughout the Western world, factories not involved in the manufacture of military trucks were turned over to the production of armaments such as shells, firearms and aero engines, while others manufactured both military vehicles and also armaments.

Many American-built trucks saw service not only in Europe but also in the Mexican border campaign of 1916, when the United States government waged war against the Mexican bandit Pancho Villa. This served as a proving ground for these trucks, many of which were later shipped to Europe

for military service. At this time, few US-built military trucks were standardized, and it was not until the development of the US Quartermaster Corps's 'B'-Class heavy truck, known as the "Liberty", that proper standardization occurred.

On the civilian front, producer-gas was used to combat the lack of petrol, and in the United States the 1916 Federal Aid Road Act was instrumental in establishing a new interstate highway system which contributed greatly to the development of American commercial vehicles. With a rubber tyre shortage, particularly in Germany where manufacturers had relied upon British- and French-made supplies, unconventional steel-wheeled vehicles, sometimes incorporating metal plates backed by small leaf springs, appeared for a short while, but these were mainly for heavy tractors used

for hauling artillery. Developments in commercial vehicle design, such as the use of shaft-drive, glass windscreens and electric rather than acetylene lighting, were now creeping in from the passenger car side and, although apparent in many light commercials, it was some years before these were adopted for the heavy commercial market. Pneumatic tyres were also becoming commonplace on lighter types but, again, were to remain a rarity on "heavies" for some time.

While the war did much to establish new standards for commercial vehicles, military vehicle requirements were far different from those used on the public highway. High payloads and economy were more important to civilian operators than high ground clearance or all-wheel drive. Thus, with a return to peace, much re-organization was necessary.

# Peacetime development

WHILE the end of the war in 1918 opened the field to new manufacturers, it also presented new problems to the existing commercial motor industry. Some German armament producers, such as Krupp, were not allowed to continue production, and had to turn to the manufacture of trucks instead. However, vast quantities of ex-military vehicles were already being released into the civilian market and snapped up by both operators and thousands of servicemen anxious to set up in the expanding goods and passenger haulage business. In France alone there were thousands of American, British and German trucks scattered around, and although there were only some 400 licensed road hauliers in the United Kingdom at this time, by 1923 these had expanded to 2400, many of the vehicles being shipped into the country through ex-army dealers. Thus, demand for new vehicles was relatively low and sales suffered badly. Some manufacturers, such as Leyland Motors, established a re-conditioning plant for ex-WD trucks, while some dealers concentrated on particular makes such as the American Peerless and FWD, ultimately constructing vehicles of similar design and using the same identity.

By this time production equipment was out-of-date, and existing manufacturers were often faced with considerable re-tooling before new models could be introduced. Most, however, continued to concentrate on existing designs until 1923, due to a considerable slump in trade whereby those manufacturers which also built passenger cars found themselves with quantities of unsold cars. Another result of war-surplus trucks flooding the market was the effect on the road-going steamer, which was pushed further into the background by legislation and, ultimately, by the development of the diesel engine.

By 1919 the American, Malcolm Loughhead, had developed the 4-wheel Lockheed hydraulic braking system, and both Dunlop and Goodyear had announced their first pneumatic tyres. There was also increasing interest in large-capacity passenger vehicles.

*Left* Special facilities, such as the roof-mounted sleeper compartment on this 3-ton White, were needed for long-distance hauls in the USA. *Centre and bottom left* Specialist British municipal vehicles were led by the 3-wheeled Lacre roadsweeper; the French market was led by the DeDion 4-wheeler. *Right* Steam was still popular and even Leyland Motors offered an "undertype" wagon until 1926. *Bottom right* Vast numbers of ex-military trucks were now rapidly replacing the horse, particularly for transporting fuel.

Such change in social conditions resulted in the gradual development of vehicles built specifically to carry passengers. Some manufacturers which had been less fortunate during the war and had concentrated on the manufacture of armaments, were forced to start again with a small selection of lightweight commercials for passengers or payloads of up to 2½ tons. Existing passenger models, such as the 34-seat AEC 'B'-Type, were replaced by designs of even greater capacity, in this instance by the 46-seat 'K'-Type, and soon after by the 54-seat 'S'-Type. By 1923 the first of the famous 'NS'-Type, with its futuristic low-loading entrance, had appeared.

By the mid-1920s, road transport was becoming established and new ideas were plentiful. Forward-control or cab-over-engine layout were popular ways of increasing the load-carrying space, and Scammell Lorries Ltd, founded in 1921, built a 7½-ton 6-wheeled articulated lorry designed by Lt Col A G Scammell, DSO, which quickly led to other vehicles of similar layout. By 1925 a new 5/6-ton Dennis load-carrier had become the first Dennis to be powered by a monobloc engine with four integrally-cast cylinders and two detachable heads. The earlier charabanc was now being replaced by the sedate motor coach, one excellent example being the Albion 'Viking' of 1923. In 1924, Thornycroft built its first unit-construction vehicle, the A1 1½-tonner with engine, clutch and gearbox mounted as one unit at three points in the chassis frame. The old leather-to-metal clutch was now replaced by a single-plate unit and pneumatic tyres fitted. Pneumatics had been regarded with some scepticism by the authorities, as had 4-wheel brakes which were not permitted in London until 1926, when a suitably equipped Dennis 'E'-Type was tested on a hard surface with a coating of soft soap.

As a contrast to the European manufacturer, where each marque had an individual identity, and many parts were manufactured by the one company, the majority of American companies built vehicles which were purely assembled, using components which were available to anybody. It was not until the 1930s that this pattern began to change.

## The rigid multi-wheeler

THE DEVELOPMENT of pneumatic tyres led to the construction of the first multi-wheeled goods and passenger models. Among the first rigid 6-wheelers were single- and double-drive conversions of the US Army's "Liberty" truck, followed by a new double-drive 4-wheel braked bogie developed by Hendrickson Mfg, of America, in 1924. With larger payloads, pneumatic-tyred 4-wheelers suffered increasingly from punctures, leading to the idea that the load should be distributed over two rear axles, with manufacturers adopting different layouts and drive systems. It was also discovered that 2-axle pneumatic-tyred bogies caused less damage to road surfaces than those of single-axle design.

Varying drive layouts were adopted for such bogies. The German Büssing organization drove each rear axle separately from an auxiliary gearbox located behind the main box, while the Scottish-built Caledon 6-wheeler had one "live" axle driving two "dead" ones by roller chain. Karrier was another British marque that was early on the 6-wheeled scene, using two under-worm axles. Guy Motors delivered the world's first 6-wheeled trolleybus to the Wolverhampton Corp in 1926, fitting a double-deck body and regenerative control. This company also built the world's first double-deck motorbus, as well as a small fleet of 6-wheeled double-deckers in 1927.

Another notable 6-wheeler was the Thornycroft A3, developed from the A1 "subsidy" lorry of 1924 and intended for cross-country operation. This was actually a military vehicle, but quickly caught on overseas where its worm-drive axles and auxiliary transmission established it as a worthwhile machine for both on- and off-road work. In military guise, the A3 could handle 1½-ton loads and, for civilian work, loads of up to 2½ tons could be managed. Cross-country tracks could be fitted over the rear wheels as required.

Meanwhile, on the passenger vehicle front, the Associated Daimler Co, formed from a short-lived liaison between Associated Equipment Co Ltd and Daimler Co Ltd, developed the

*Above* The bonneted 4-wheeled arrangement was still preferred in Europe as on this 1922 Austrian-built Steyr street-washer. *Top* Rugby Trucks catered for the smaller end of the light-weight truck market. *Centre* Articulation meant greater capacity, an ideal solution for household removals, this operator is using a Magiruz-hauled outfit. *Above right and right* Multi-wheeled rigids were gaining in popularity on both sides of the Atlantic, demonstrated here by a 1929 Scammell 'Rigid-6' and in 1924 by a Mack "Bulldog". *Far right* Breweries were among the last strongholds of steam, this 6-ton Foden was delivered to the Openshaw Brewery Ltd in 1928.

massive Model 802 or "London Six", using a double-reduction worm bogie similar to that used in a 10-ton goods model produced by Brozincevic & Co, Zürich. The "London Six" was a breakthrough in that engine vibration was minimized by mounting the 6-cyl sleeve-valve unit in a subframe which was supported in the main chassis frame by a series of cushion pads, with final-drive effected by a central under-slung worm-gear for each wheel and each axle's own differential.

By this time, the bonneted layout was the most popular for both goods and passenger models, and while some truck manufacturers shifted their allegiance to passenger cars, so others switched from cars to trucks, or added trucks to their product lines. One such was Morris Cars Ltd, which set up Morris Commercial Cars Ltd in 1924 to build a new 1-tonner, adding 1½- and 2-ton double-drive 6-wheelers within three years.

Many countries, such as Japan and the Soviet Union, were new to commercial vehicle manufacture, but were quick to develop reliable new models, often based on existing British or American designs. Indeed, it was Britain and America which set the example to many other countries, particularly with operating commercials, for in Britain alone, between 1919 and 1929, the number of operational goods vehicles rose from 62,000 to 330,000, and in America these figures were even higher.

Six-cyl petrol engines were now making their mark, the first 6-cyl Leyland commercial being the 'Titan' double-decker announced in 1927. The 'Titan' was also one of the first lowbridge double-deckers, with a sunken gangway in each saloon and an overall height of less than 4m. One of the most talked-about exhibits in 1927 was the Thornycroft 'Lightning' motor coach with a new side-valve

6-cyl petrol engine producing 70bhp. Some argued it was well ahead of its time, having vacuum-assisted 4-wheel brakes, but it merely pointed the way for other manufacturers.

Advances in these fields precipitated other changes. At Tilling-Stevens, petrol-electric propulsion was replaced by petrol power, with the introduction of the lightweight 4-cyl 'Express' passenger model, and by 1926 the world's first frameless tank semi-trailer had been pioneered by Scammell Lorries Ltd, Watford, Herts. By the end of the 1920s, the military lorry was rapidly disappearing in passenger and goods haulage circles. In 1928 the first oil-engined truck to enter service in the United Kingdom was a Mercedes-Benz, and one year later the Kerr-Stuart, the first all-British diesel lorry, arrived. Also in 1929, two of the world's heaviest vehicles, 100-ton Scammells, were constructed for heavy haulage work.

# The depression

THE 1930s dawned with the Depression hanging over the world. Its influence meant that manufacturers and operators were beginning to use the diesel engine for motor vehicles, because it was more economical.

Diesel engines had been fitted experimentally in certain commercials from the mid-1920s, one of the first British examples being fitted to a London bus in 1928, but it was on the Continent that such developments grew, with Berliet of France fitting its first diesel in 1930, Renault in 1931, and Fiat of Italy in 4- and 6-tonners in 1931. Leyland Motors was also experimenting with diesel, and the Tilling-Stevens Express bus was offered with a 4-cyl diesel engine, but the first complete diesel-engined bus built in the United Kingdom was a 1931 Crossley.

Many of these engines were constructed along similar lines, but there were exceptions. Klockner-Humboldt-Deutz was looking at air-cooled units, but these were not fitted in any quantity until 1940. In the United States, both Cummins and General Motors (GM) were experimenting, the former fitting its first diesel, the Model 'H', to a truck in 1932, while GM pondered on the development of a 2-stroke diesel which did not go into full production until 1937.

While it was apparent that the diesel engine was the answer to the economic problem, many operators were still prejudiced as it was largely an unknown quantity.

Although some American manufacturers were developing diesel engines, there were others concentrating on the development of more powerful petrol units, as the United States had a plentiful supply of cheap home-produced petrol. Thus, the petrol engine dominated the field in the United States until the 1960s, when increasing dependency upon imported fuels led to an increased use of automotive diesels. Similarly, Germany relied upon imported fuel, and Hitler was quick to realize the importance of developing the country's own fuel source. Thus, diesel came to the fore.

Generally, there were two types of diesel engine – direct and indirect injection – although most were of the in-

direct type, as this was quieter and more economical. The advent of the diesel engine brought new-found wealth to many established concerns.

Fodens Ltd, of Sandbank, Cheshire, also went through considerable re-organization at this time with E R Foden and his son leaving the company to set up the diesel vehicle manufacturer ERF Ltd in 1933. Meanwhile Fodens itself continued vehicle building, changing from steam to diesel propulsion. Dennis Bros Ltd, of Guildford, Surrey, moved into the diesel field in 1935, with a version of its Lancet II passenger model powered by a Dennis Big Four petrol engine or a Dennis-Lanova low-compression diesel. One of the earliest diesel engine builders in Britain was W H Dorman & Co Ltd, whose first design was a 4-cyl job developing 20bhp at 1000rpm. This company built

*Above* The early 1930s were a crucial time for the California-based Fageol Motors Co, despite the production of short bonneted trucks with a low centre of gravity. *Left* When this Type 85 Alfa-Romeo was built in 1934 even bonneted trucks were beginning to reflect more modern styling. *Bottom left* The first passenger vehicle to carry the Bedford name was the 14-seater WHB built in 1931. *Top right* The 2½-ton FN was built in Belgium, powered by a straight 8 petrol engine. *Above middle right* The spoked wheels on this 1932 Kenworth were unusual for a vehicle operating on the west side of the US at this time. *Above bottom right* The Sentinel was one of the most advanced steam vehicles and the most famous was the multi-wheeled 58 of 1934. *Right* 'Commercial Car Journal' was now the leading road transport publication in the USA.

both the Dorman-Ricardo high-speed airless injection type and the direct-injection type, but in recent years has concentrated on the manufacture of industrial diesels rather than those for automotive use. Another firm which is synonymous with the production of automotive diesels is F Perkins Ltd, Peterborough, which was founded in 1932 to produce the P6 diesel, again popular as a conversion.

However, it was not just diesel developments which accelerated during the 1930s, as commercial bodywork was improving rapidly, particularly on the passenger vehicle side. Motor coach bodies throughout Europe and America were following passenger car styling, particularly in Germany, and ventilation and other comforts were much improved. Many coaches had sunshine roofs which could be folded back for all-weather

*Right* The Latil 'Traulier' was a French design combining the manouevrability of 4-wheel steering with the go-anywhere characteristics of 4-wheel drive. *Below right* Morris-Commercial's 3-ton C9/60, although of bonneted layout, had its engine protruding into the cab giving it a "snub-nosed" appearance. *Below* Legislation was now forcing breweries to change from steam to diesel, by going with this trend manufacturers such as Foden (whose logo appears below) managed to retain their customers.

operation, and both buses and coaches were far more comfortable.

By the mid-1930s, with the exception of trolleybuses, 6-wheeled passenger models were vanishing while 4-axle rigid goods models were offered by most British diesel-engined goods vehicle manufacturers. The use of articulated load-carriers was catching on, and in the United States, the first "double bottoms" – articulated vehicles with an extra drawbar trailer – were beginning to appear on the longer inter-state routes. In urban areas, there was the "mechanical horse", a strange 3-wheeled tractor replacing the horse and cart, built mainly in Britain by Scammell and Karrier. This vehicle was specially devised to hitch up to horse-drawn carts, particularly used by railway companies to speed deliveries. A derivative of this was the 3-wheeled Ford Tug of 1935, which had a Model 'Y' van body.

A bonneted layout was still the norm for heavy commercials but forward-control was becoming increasingly popular, due to the fact that more load-carrying space was now available.

However, a generally conservative attitude ensured that the bonnet-

*Top left* German manufacturers were now well ahead, both in vehicle design and in the development of new propulsion systems. This Magirus-Deutz had an underfloor engine running on producer gas. *Middle left above* The Czechoslovakian Tatra T82 6-wheeler of 1936 had an air-cooled diesel engine. *Above* Aerodynamic styling became the vogue in North America and Canada at this time. Labart's Canadian brewery took delivery of this spectacular White in 1937. *Left* The ERF C1561 6-wheeler had a 5-cylinder Gardner diesel engine and was popular with many British hauliers during the 1930s and 1940s.

ed arrangement would continue for some time. As the distance between delivery points increased, so the use of sleeper cabs grew, mainly on the Continent and in the United States, and to make the driver's job even easier, power-steering began to appear. Suspensions were improved, some incorporating rubber units, and brake systems were up-dated to make the heavier trucks, buses and coaches safer.

Hydraulic braking was offered on many 4-wheeled rigids, although multi-wheeled rigids and artics were still without brakes on some axles. In Switzerland, Italy and France, the first exhaust brakes, suited to mountainous terrains, began to appear, and in America particularly, automatic or semi-automatic transmissions were being fitted.

In common with passenger body-

work, truck bodies were beginning to be constructed of light-alloy, and some American manufacturers were even building truck and van bodies on line-flow principles. Also in America, increasing use was being made of lightweight materials, even in chassis manufacture, and by the end of the 1930s most of the present-day leading truck and bus manufacturers were in business.

# World war II

THROUGHOUT the latter half of the 1930s, the world was relentlessly moving towards another war. The German Schell Programme of 1938 called for the standardization of military truck production, segregating vehicles into light-, medium- and heavy-duty types from 1 to 6½ tons payload with engines of a given minimum output. These ideas were later reflected in the commercial truck boom of the 1950s and 1960s when German-built trucks had to have a minimum of 8bhp per ton of a vehicle's gross weight.

By 1939 the German forces were prepared for hostilities. While many hard lessons had been learned during World War I, some countries were still lagging behind in vehicle production. In Britain, production of military vehicles and equipment was stepped up towards the end of the 1930s, although many military trucks were merely militarized versions of commercial models. The larger manufacturers, such as Leyland Motors, moved into armaments production, while others, such as Austin and Morris-Commercial, concentrated on trucks and artillery tractors.

Weight did not matter as much as the vehicle's ability to go anywhere, and sturdily constructed 4 x 4, 6 x 4 and 6 x 6 trucks were rushed off the production lines. One British manufacturer which was prepared was Guy Motors, Wolverhampton, which had abandoned civilian in favour of government contracts in the mid-1930s, concentrating on production of the 4-wheel drive 'Quad-Ant', an 8 x 8 load-carrier, and, after 1941, a civilian version of the 'Quad-Ant' known as the 'Vixen'. The best known 3-ton army trucks were to be the Bedford QL 4 x 4 and 'OY'-Series 4 x 2, of which, at the time, nearly 1000 a week were being built. Both Commer and Karrier also built 4 x 4s, but perhaps the most well remembered of the period were the 4 x 4 AEC Matador medium artillery tractor and the massive Scammell Pioneer range of artillery, tank recovery and vehicle breakdown models based on Scammell Lorries' pre-war oilfield and heavy haulage tractor.

Although British and American forces moved their tanks by road on

*Above* The Morris-Commercial C8 was one of the most prolific field artillery tractors on the Allied side.
*Left* German Forces were great users of the hybrid half-truck. This was the 2-ton Magirus-Deutz 53000/SSM.
*Left bottom:* A 1943 Bedford QL, which was one of the most familiar 3-ton 4 x 4's in the British Services.

*Top and extreme right* Two US truck advertisements. The competitive nature of many US truck advertisements turned to propaganda at the end of the 1930s as World War II got under way. *Right* Diamond T production lines, showing part of the "Six-by-Six" and "Tank-hauler" production. Diamond T's war truck production exceeds the normal peacetime heavy-truck output of the entire automotive industry.

*Top right* The austere Fiat 626N
3-tonner of 1939 was used by
civilians as well as by the Armed
Forces. *Far right middle* The
Model 1506 cab fitted to civvy
GMC's in 1941 was plain to say the
least. *Extreme far right middle* Due
to the vast numbers of vehicles
needed, many US manufacturers
built vehicles of standard design.
This Mormon-Herrington
H-542-11 5-ton tractor was based
on International Harvester
designs. *Far bottom right* This
AEC 'Mammoth Major III' was
supplied in 1941 for essential
civilian use. *Right* An Austin K4
(16) which was used in peacetime
as a coal truck.

transporters, thereby causing them much wear and tear, the Germans preferred to use rail. The Allies also perfected the movement of other heavy loads and, with a return to peace, adapted these methods to the haulage and construction industries, often using ex-military equipment. Articulation was used, particularly for hauling aircraft components such as wings and fuselages, and Scammell Lorries again came to the fore in the supply of general cargo or tank semi-trailers with automatic couplings.

One American-built truck worthy of special mention was the 6 x 6 GMC of which more than 600,000 were built. This became a real army work-horse and was adopted for a surprising number of tasks. There were many much heavier types as well, such as those produced by Autocar, Diamond T, Kenworth, Oshkosh, Reo and White, as well as numerous lighter types.

Although much of the world's truck production was given over to military types, civilian models were still being built. In France, for example, Berliet was producing wood-burning trucks which ran on the gas resulting from the combustion process but this ended with the Occupation, when manufacturers were forced to supply vehicles to the German forces. However, it was the French heavy vehicle industry that was hardest hit by World War II, although Allied bombers also left little of the German truck plants standing.

By 1941 fuel shortages were a serious problem throughout Europe. Even bus operators could not obtain sufficient supplies, and many of these vehicles were withdrawn, while others were converted to operate with producer-gas trailers. Some single-deckers even ran on town gas stored in huge tent-like structures mounted on the roof. A year later certain manufacturers, such as Guy Motors, were authorized to build austerity versions of their passenger models to replace pre-war vehicles wrecked or damaged. To clear bomb damage or haul heavy machinery, traction engines and other extinct types were moved into service.

# Off road & construction vehicles

Following World War I many hundreds of all-wheel drive and other heavy specification military trucks came onto the civilian market and were quickly snapped up by the construction industry and others requiring heavy-duty vehicles. New civilian versions were soon developed for on/off-road working and even larger strictly off-road types gradually developed, principally for mining and quarrying. The most common off-road types are now dump trucks. There are other designs which have been developed specifically for the building and construction industries; these include drilling rigs, lorry-mounted cranes and concrete mixers.

3

1

2

8

9

1 The twin-engined rotary snowplough built around 1920 by the Winther Motor Truck Co, Wisconsin was unusual for its day. 2 A 1919 Walker Model 'K' 1-ton battery-electric integral van. 3 The front-discharge unit is an increasingly popular feature. In the case of the 'B'-Series Oshkosh it incorporated a rear-mounted engine, a centrally placed one-man cab and a 6x6 layout. 4 Off-highway dump trucks such as this rear-wheel drive Terex 33-11B are the real construction giants. 5 This 6x6 Autocar construction truck, made by the White Motor Corp. can cope with very heavy work. 6/7 The 'Lowline' crane carrier is of almost universal appeal, it is exemplified here by the Mitsubishi Fuso K600 60-tonner.

8/9 An early prototype Scammell 'Pioneer' equipped with all-over tracks shows off its capabilities while Scammell's first tank transporter recovers a disabled truck. 10 The British-built AIM 'Stalwart' 6x6 with full independent suspension and steering on all but the last two wheels was adopted by the military authorities of many countries as a standard amphibious land-carrier. 11 The US-built NOZ Mack of the 1940s was a 7½-ton 6x6 with double-reduction gearing in the steering ends of the front axle which provided a higher front axle than the vehicle's hubs.

# The post-war years

THE WESTERN WORLD of 1945 was far different from that of 1919. Not only was there a shortage of materials (the most important being steel), but also monetary restrictions out-of-date equipment, and a lack of skilled labour. In the United Kingdom, the government decided to increase exports, and insisted that sixty percent of total vehicle exports should comprise commercial vehicles. By 1946 the government's seemingly impossible sales figures had been reached, simply by selling more vehicles abroad than before the war.

British manufacturers continued mainly with pre-war ranges, such as the bonneted Commer 'Superpoise', launched in 1939, and the Bedford 'O'-Type, also a normal-control design. This gave firms sufficient breathing space to introduce totally new models like the forward-control underfloor-engined Commer of 1948, and the 'Big Bedford' of 1950. This had a 4.9-litre 6-cyl petrol engine, regarded by many as the best petrol engine ever fitted in a commercial.

The 1947 British Transport Act led to the nationalization of road haulage, which in turn resulted in fleet standardization and other improvements. By 1948, United Kingdom commercial vehicle exports were five times higher than in 1938, and British expertise led

the world. Leyland engines and other components were used in the first DAF trucks and many United Kingdom manufacturers, particularly the premium truck and bus builders like Fodens, Atkinson, ERF and Leyland, concentrated on Commonwealth markets, such as Northern and Southern Rhodesia, South Africa and Australia. Mergers became commonplace in an effort to consolidate activities, with AEC acquiring Crossley in 1948 and Maudslay in 1949, while Leyland bought Albion in 1951, and Scammell in 1955.

The Japanese now have one of the world's largest vehicle industries, certainly as far as exports are concerned, but in 1946 it was still in its infancy. Hino's first truck was a 15-ton capacity artic announced in 1946, followed one year later by an air-braked articulated bus. Volume production did not get underway until 1949, the company's heaviest model being a 6 x 6 10-tonner introduced in 1951. During these early days of the Japanese motor industry there were close ties with European manufacturers such as Renault and Rootes, but once established in their own right, these ties were quickly broken.

The immediate post-war period was the heyday of the American truck-building industry, with products being

*Far left and top left* For countries that had been involved in the war, many post-war models were the same as pre-war types. Both the Foden DG6/15 and the Belford 'M'-type fall into this category. *Bottom left* After the war Leyland developed a number of all-steel cabs with forward-control such as this 'Beaver'. *Above* The 'KB'-Line International of 1947 was a much modified and improved version of the pre-war 'K'-Series. *Right* In 1950 GMC announced a new "weight-saving" diesel tractor which used much more light alloy than before.

GMC TRUCKS

*Far right* The WF800 Freightliner
"cabover", designed by a truck
operator became the White
Freightliner when White took over
Freightliner sales and service in
1951. Meanwhile, the White
Motor Co's own idea of a
medium-weight "cabover" was
the tiltcab '3000' series. *Right and
below* Peterbilt
and Kenworth were custom-
building their heavy-duty
"conventionals".

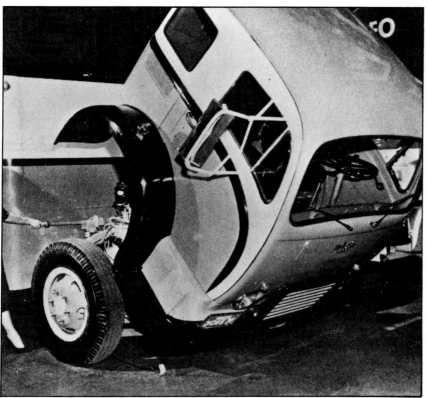

sold worldwide. It was at this time that American manufacturers set the trend for heavy "cabover" articulated tractor units for long-distance haulage, employing many ideas gleaned from the war years and, in particular, from aircraft production. Aluminium alloy was being used in increasing quantities, not only for components but also for body sections and framing. Some of the larger manufacturers were even acquiring individual body-building concerns, so that vehicle bodies, such as light- and mediumweight panel vans, could be produced by that manufacturer.

Since World War II there have been two major innovations in the commercial vehicle field. One is the almost universal adoption of articulation, and the other the use of forward-control tilt-cabs. Articulation has now developed furthest in the United States where, since the 1950s, "double-bottom" outfits comprising one tractor, a dolly and two semi-trailers, have become common. In Europe a drawbar configuration is still the most popular, whilst articulation rates as the most popular method in the United Kingdom.

The use of forward-control tilt-cabs in the United States only really caught on in the 1950s, before which time bonneted tractors were more popular. However, the "cabover" layout permits longer semi-trailers to be used, thereby making vehicle operations more economical.

## New technology

WITH A WORLDWIDE INCREASE in prosperity, the accent was placed on vehicle design, although great advances were still being made in other aspects of vehicle manufacture, particularly their efficiency. At the 1948 Commercial Motor Show, Fodens Ltd exhibited a new 4-cyl 2-stroke diesel engine which was to herald a new technological age for the commercial vehicle. It was a particularly efficient design, followed in 1955 by a 3-cyl Rootes 2-stroke for diesel or multi-fuel applications. Turbocharged diesels were first used in trucks by Volvo of Sweden, where gross weights are

*Far right top* **A 1953 Volvo L375 4/5 ton truck.** *Middle top* **In spite of being functional, the bonneted French Willème was a decidedly ugly vehicle.** *Right top* **Built in France in 1955 this Latil was unlikely to be seen outside France.** *Right* **The 1956 bonneted Bedford was a very versatile truck that did much to boost Britain's export figures.** *Below* **This crew-cabbed petrol-engined Dennis was typical of the vehicles operated by many British local authorities at the time.**

the highest in Europe. Instead of building larger engines to produce greater power, Volvo fitted a turbo compressor which enabled as much as fifty percent more power to be produced by each engine. This system was announced in 1954 and, as well as giving increased power output, offers low fuel consumption and quiet running.

Petrol engines were still popular in the United States after World War II, but as the 1950s progressed, the use of diesels in heavy trucks became the norm. Mack Trucks announced its 'Thermodyne' diesel in 1953, and by the early 1960s many British-built Perkins diesels were being fitted in even light- and mediumweight delivery models, and high-speed 'V'-form diesels were being used both in the United States and Europe. Agreements were signed between the American-owned Cummins Engine Co, Jaguar in the United Kingdom, and Krupp in Germany, to manufacture Cummins engines in Europe under the Jaguar-Cummins and Krupp-Cummins brand names. These agreements, however, were later cancelled and Cummins 'V' engines built in quantity in the company's British plant. While some, such as Cummins and Scania, have developed successful 'V' diesels, others have not. AEC, Southall, Middx, developed its own V8 unit, known as the '800'-Series, but this was unsuccessful.

# The new era

During the 1960s there was considerable interest in the use of gas-turbine power for both trucks and buses, and a number of prototypes were built. Many of the leading American manufacturers investigated this source of power and in the United Kingdom, British Leyland developed four vehicles. However, with the exception of the massive Lectra-Haul dump truck, which is powered by an 1100bhp Saturn gas-turbine, none of these reached production stage and the cost of fuel is now prohibitive.

Recent years have seen the opening up of large areas of the world to long-distance trucking largely due to the construction of motorways and other major routes. The Asian Highway was just one example, having a considerable effect on European road haulage and, eventually, on the design of vehicles operating over long distances. Many manufacturers began offering a special "Middle East" package on heavier trucks and tractor units, with features which provided maximum driver comfort. Vehicle braking systems and tyres have improved as distances and speeds have increased, so that the modern long-haul artic unit invariably relies upon full air brakes, while intermediate types have adopted air/hydraulic systems. More recently, exhaust brakes and other forms of engine retarder have appeared more frequently.

*Left* Scammell's 'Highwayman' was particularly popular as an artic tanker, special versions of it were frequently sold abroad. This one was sold to Venezuela. *Bottom far left* The Mercedes-Benz artic truck was popular in the UK in the 60s.

It was a bonneted model and had forward-control. *Bottom centre* A mini revolution in the UK cab design resulted in some very pleasing models. ERF's 'LV' cab was a case in point. *Bottom right* This mass-produced Ford Thames 'Trader' was now a familiar sight on British roads.

Truck transmissions have also changed. It is only since the war that synchromesh transmissions have appeared in large numbers, and by the early 1960s range-change transmissions and 2-speed axles were increasingly popular. Automatic or semi-automatic transmissions also have their place, but have never gained much popularity in the truck field. On the suspension front, air systems have become commonplace on passenger models but are still comparatively rare on trucks, being more popular for vehicles carrying bulk liquids than on those for general goods.

A further revolution in road transport has been created by the movement of containers on an international scale and the use of special pallets to aid mechanical handling. As recently as the 1960s, truck drivers had to load, sheet and rope their own vehicles, and some still do, but in the main the loads are now containerized or palletized, simplifying the operation considerably. In some countries, such as France, even the semi-trailers are specially built to be carried on "Kangaroo" rail wagons, thereby eliminating long trips by road, but in the main, containers of standard dimensions are used internationally, enabling complete interchangeability.

*Left* British trucks for the Australian market were very different from their UK counterparts, roadtrains such as this AEC 'Mammoth Major' hauled outfit being commonplace in the outback. *Centre left* Concentrating on custom-built trucks, the Hendrickson Mfg. Co. Illinois, offered its Model 'B' tipper to virtually any specification. *Centre right* At the heavier end of the UK market was the Thorneycroft 'Antor' C6T. It sold to military and heavy haulage customers, this example being exported to Argentina. *Bottom left* By the end of the decade AB Volvo was expanding rapidly in export fields. Despite the dated appearance of this bonetted range it was well suited for this market. *Bottom centre* The Hino 'T.E.' – F series tipper of 1966 was another very straightforward design. *Bottom right* American regulations permit the use of double and triple-bottom long-haul outfits such as this GMC 'Astro' machine.

# The present and the future

THE 1970s could be truly termed the technological age as far as the commercial vehicle is concerned. We have already seen how the gas-turbine was seriously considered at the end of the previous decade as an alternative to petrol or diesel power for the heavier vehicle and how this possibility was brought to an abrupt halt by the fuel crisis. Meanwhile, in a further attempt to produce an economical substitute fuel for use in road vehicles, experiments got under way in most countries into the feasibility of battery-electric propulsion, the major obstacle being that of weight. Leaders in this field are General Motors in the USA and the Lucas-Chloride partnership in the UK, although a recent announcement from British Rail's Technical Centre in Derby suggests that they may at last have developed a lightweight sodium-sulphur battery suitable for road use.

The last decade has also seen increasing interest in the protection of the environment which has frequently backfired on the road transport operator in the form of lorry cordons and other restrictive legislation. From the bureaucratic angle, the EEC (Common Market) has also had much effect throughout Europe, making the tachograph ( 'spy in the cab' ) compulsory in member countries and reducing permissible driving hours. Connected both with this and the environmentalists' attitude, there have also been attempts, largely unsuccessful, to transfer goods from road to rail. Certain European countries no longer permit heavy trucks to operate on Sundays, substituting instead a railway service on which all lorries are carried.

In many countries the weights and size of vehicles has gradually increased and in Britain experiments are being conducted with American-style double-bottom outfits, comprising tractor, semi-trailer, drawbar dolly and second semi-trailer, for motorway operation. Abnormal and indivisible loads have also become heavier, with some European specialists now offering a transport service for individual loads in excess of 500 tons.

There have been even more changes in the manufacturing side of

*Above left* By the early 1970s "Big Red", Ford of America's gas-turbine prototype, was becoming a thing of the past rather than the future. *Above* The EEC introduced UK truckers to tachographs. These record drivers' hours and the vehicle operations. They were phased in gradually towards the end of the 70s. *Left* MAN's giant X-90 project with roof-mounted sleeping compartments looks to the future. *Below* The oil crisis of the mid-1970s inspired this prototype of a wedge-shaped Paymaster. It was designed by an Oregon trucker. *Right* Chevrolet's 'Turbo Titan III', a gas-turbine powered aerodynamically styled vehicle whose low silhouette provided low wind resistance.

the business, with some old-established concerns taken over and sometimes even closed down completely. A classic example is that of British Leyland which had already acquired the manufacturing plants for AEC, Albion, Bristol, Guy, Scammell and Thornycroft, discontinuing all except Bristol and Scammell, by the end of the 1970s. In America, meanwhile, Daimler-Benz AG of Germany has acquired the Freightliner Corp and, subject to confirmation, AB Volvo of Sweden has purchased the huge White Motor Corp, taking over assembly of

*Top* The cab on the Berlet-derived TR305 is also used by Ford on its 'Transcontinental' model. *Above* As continental manufacturers moved in on the British market so new models gradually emerged to please UK operators. A DAF offering is the rigid-8 2300. *Right* Volvos have been built to survive the arduous weather conditions of Scandinavia, so it is not surprising that the heavier models with their rugged specifications have carved a niche for themselves in long-haul transport operations in other parts of the world. European operators using the F88 and F89 ranges led the field in the race to North Africa, the Middle East, and beyond in the mid-1970s.

# Custom rigs

Originating mainly in the United States, the custom rig is gradually spreading throughout the Western World, particularly among owner drivers. Special paint jobs and the fitting of chromed accessories are essential to the custom rig operator who, through these means, is able to express his individuality. There is now such a demand for this that virtually all US truck manufacturers now offer special paint schemes, following the lead set by companies such as Freightliner, Kenworth, Mack and Peterbilt, many of whose sales are aimed at the owner driver. Custom paint shops now also cater for trucks.

*Top* An imaginative 'cowboy' image is carried by this White Western Star. *Above* These two White Western Star tractors show just how far some manufacturers are prepared to go. *Far left* This fancy Kenworth "conventional" is definitely not ex-factory. *Left* These Kenworth paint jobs were specially developed for the owner-operator.

White, Autocar and Western Star trucks. These moves have been brought about by the search for still wider markets by European manufacturers.

Passenger transportation has also altered in the last decade, particularly in Britain. By the end of the 1960s the familiar half-cab double-decker which had been the mainstay of British bus operations for many years, was no longer in production, being superseded by mainly rear-engined full-front models easily adapted for one-man operation. As in the truck business, Britain's bus fleets were gradually infiltrated by similar vehicles of Continental origin, notably the Metro-Scania and Volvo 'Ailsa'.

For many years the articulated single-decker for fast urban operation had been popular in Europe and Scandinavia, especially in Germany and Sweden, and as in the case of the double-bottom goods vehicle, the British authorities permitted experiments with these on public roads. Similar arrangements were made in the USA, again using imported European models, and the idea is now being adopted almost worldwide with MAN, Scania and Volvo in the forefront.

In common with most other manufacturing industries, the world's commercial vehicle industry has suffered badly from the economic recession of the last few years. Some new marques, such as Ginaf, Stonefield, Terberg and Titan, have appeared during this time but even some of these have experienced financial problems. There is little doubt that the recession will have a continuing effect upon both commercial vehicle manufacturing and operating and some will find their only course is to close down. While this situation prevails, significant developments are likely to be few unless in the cause of economy. In the face of the gradual erosion of the world's oil resources, the search for new fuels will certainly continue, but there remains much development work to be done in this field.

The quest for fuel economy and more power has seen various developments in the engine field. In the USA, where petrol-engined trucks were the norm at the end of the 1960s, the diesel now reigns supreme, the cost of petrol being largely prohibitive. American truck operations have also been affected by a blanket 55mph speed limit, again in the interests of economy. In Europe, meanwhile, the fixed-head diesel engine gained brief popularity as a maintenance-free unit, only to fall down on length of operational life, but turbo-charging, largely pioneered by AB Volvo, is obviously here to stay. 'V'-configuration engines are particularly popular in Germany where Mercedes and Magirus are the leaders.

*Top far left* The Scottish-built Ailsa double-decker, with Volvo components, illustrated the British approach to urban transit operations. *Top centre left* The 'juggernaut' syndrome of the 1970s encouraged Mercedes to develop a less imposing heavy truck cab without sacrificing its capabilities. *Left* This early model of Leyland's 'Roadtrain' (built in 1980), the 16-28 incorporated many components that can be adapted for virtually any size or weight of vehicle. *Centre far left* The Maxeter 'Flexibus' which uses Mercedes running gears. *Centre left* For basic ruggedness Scammell's 'Crusader' became the general haulage vehicle of the early 1970s, often carrying a sleeper car which makes it suitable for long-distance work. *Bottom far left* The 1978 Fiat truck range illustrates the marque's design similarities which could lead to more economic production. *Bottom centre* West coast styling from General Motors in this GMC 'General'. *Below* Kenworth continued to build West coach types, both ''cabovers'' and ''conventionals''.

# Golden oldies

Because of the numerous changes in truck and bus safety legislation over the years the 'oldie' in its original form is often unacceptable as a roadworthy vehicle. However, these vehicles can be adapted to meet new regulations and have often been successfully modified.

Vehicle recovery specialists and travelling showmen are among those who have appreciated the potential of the 'oldie', often through necessity rather than choice. They have converted ex-military and cheap commercially operated designs and adapted them, for their own use to today's standards. Through working and caring for their vehicle they will have found out a great deal about it.

1 After World War II the ex-Service AEC 'Matador' 0853 4x4 became one of the best known recovery vehicles in Europe. 2 A 1950 Freightliner (foreground) and a 1940 'E'-Series Mack (behind) still in use in 1963. 3 Even this semi forward-control Mack is now in the 'oldie' class.

4 A fleet of AEC's, some of them Maudslays in disguise used by fairground people in the early 1960's. 5 With its custom paint job this ex-Services Mack NOZ 6x6 carried a fairground organ inside its restored timber body. 6 In 1952 a typical East coast offering was the 'conventional' Diamond T, another type that outlived many of its competitors. 7 The Gardner-engined Foden 'DG' range, typified by this 1939 DG6/15, survived longer than most types.

# Pioneers

**AUSTIN, Herbert** *(1866-1941)*
Herbert Austin was born at Little Missenden, Bucks, in November 1866 and by 1883 had emigrated to Australia where he became an engineering manager. In 1890 he returned to the British Isles and took up an appointment as Director of the Wolseley Sheep-Shearing Co, Birmingham, designing this company's first motorcar, a 3-wheeler, in 1895. The first 4-wheeler, also designed by Austin, appeared in 1900 and by 1906 he had set up his own production facility in the Longbridge Works, Birmingham, developing this into the huge Austin Motor Co Ltd.

Knighted in 1917 and a Conservative MP from 1919 until 1924, Austin became a baron in 1936. He died at Bromsgrove, Worcs, in May 1941.

Carl F. Benz

**BENZ, Carl F** *(1844-1929)*
Carl Friedrich Benz was born in 1844 at Karlsruhe, Germany, and his early career was as a mechanical engineer. In 1883 he founded Benz & Cie at Mannheim to build stationary internal combustion engines, designing and constructing the world's first practical internal combustion engined motor car which first ran early in 1885 and was patented in January 1886.

In 1893 Benz built his first 4-wheeled car and introduced the first of a series of racing cars in 1899. By 1906 he had left the firm to set up C Benz Söhne, Laden burg, with sons Eugen and Richard. He died on 4 April 1929.

**BOLLEE, Amédée père** *(1844-1917)*
Amédée Bollée Snr, born in 1844, ran the family bell-founding business in Le Mans, France, but was inspired by certain steam-powered exhibits at the Paris World Exhibition in 1867 to construct a fast private carriage, establishing a motor vehicle workshop in a corner of the foundry. The machine was far in advance

Amédée Bollée Snr

of anything that had gone before, following its own design parameters rather than those of horse-drawn or rail-borne vehicles.

He next constructed two 4-wheel drive 4-wheel steer tramcars with independent suspension and followed these with a new steam carriage with engine ahead of the driver and boiler at the rear. This he exhibited at the 1878 Paris World Exhibition, setting up a new workshop outside the family bell foundry, but a royalty agreement with a German manufacturer was unsuccessful and the collapse of this business led to Bollée's gradual disinterest in vehicle-building. He reverted to bell-founding, passing all vehicle enquiries to his eldest son, also Amédée Bollée.

**BOLLEE, Amédée** *fils (1868-1926)*
Amédée Bollée Jnr was just 18 when his father passed a steam carriage order to him. He had already built a light 2-seater for himself but this new project was a 16-seat double mail coach for the Marquis de Brox. He was not very successful in the steam sphere but opted instead for the petrol-driven motor car, the first of which he constructed in 1896, his designs being built under licence by De Dietrich.

He regularly took part in speed trials and this experience taught him the importance of aerodynamics. He built a number of machines with unusual torpedo-shaped bodies which led to numerous orders. By 1900 he had withdrawn from speed events and was concentrating instead on the construction of refined limited-production vehicles.

**BOLLEE, Leon** *(1870-1913)*
Amédée Bollée Jnr's younger brother, Léon, concentrated on the development of automatic machinery until the age of 26, showing one of the earliest automatic calculating machines at the 1889 Paris Exhibition. However, 1896 saw a new 3-wheeled motorcar which was the first vehicle to

be sold with pneumatic tyres as standard. Examples were built in England as well as France but within three years a new Léon Bollée design was under construction in the Darracq factory.

From 1903 Léon started to manufacture his own vehicles, backed financially and thus securely by the Vanderbilt family. Although he died in 1913, the Léon Bollée range continued for some years.

**CHRYSLER, Walter P** *(1875-1940)*
Walter Percy Chrysler was born at Wamego, Kansas, in 1875 and was later apprenticed to the Union Pacific Railroad machine shop. Joining the American Locomotive Co, he worked up to the position of Plant Manager but seeing opportunities elsewhere became Works Manager at the Buick Motor Co for half the salary. By 1916 he was President, building the Buick operation into the strongest of all General Motors subsidiaries by the time he left in 1919.

Six months later he took over the helm of both the Willys-Overland Co and the Maxwell Motor Co. These formed the basis of the Chrysler Corp, founded in 1925, which quickly introduced his own design of high-compression engined car. This became so successful that Maxwell production was discontinued.

In 1928 Chrysler purchased the Dodge Bros Manufacturing Co from the bank that had controlled it since the Dodge brothers' deaths, enabling him to launch the Plymouth range in 1928 as a new competitor for both Ford and Chevrolet.

Amédée Bollée Jnr

**CITROEN, Andre G** *(1878-1935)*
André Gustave Citroën, born in Paris on 5 February 1878, was both an engineer and an industrialist who was strongly in favour of Henry Ford's mass-production techniques, himself boosting Mors car and commercial production from 125 to 1200 units per year. He even convinced the French

Army that mass-production of munitions was essential during World War I and he set up a factory to do just this, later converting the plant into an automotive works. Refusing to admit defeat during the Depression, he introduced the only popular front-wheel drive car of the day. The company was made bankrupt in 1934 and Citroën lost control, dying in July 1935.

**DAIMLER, Gottlieb W** *(1834-1900)*
Gottlieb Wilhelm Daimler was born at Schorndorf, Württemburg, in 1834, and like Carl Benz became a mechanical engineer and inventor. At 38 he joined Eugen Langen and Nikolaus Otto at the Deutz Works in Cologne to assist with the development of a 4-stroke petrol engine. He soon became a leading figure in automotive development, setting up a workshop at Canstatt with Wilhelm Maybach in 1882 and pat-

Léon Bollée

enting one of the world's first high-speed internal combustion engines in December 1883, following this with a new design of carburettor.

In 1885 Daimler developed one of the world's first motorcycles, a 4-wheeled self-propelled carriage in 1886, a boat in 1887 and a 4-wheeled motorcar in 1889. The French rights to his engine patents were sold to Panhard et Levassor and in 1890 he founded Daimler-Motoren-Gesellschaft, again at Canstatt, to produce more motor vehicles, one of which was the Mercedes car, named after Co-Director Émile Jellinek's daughter. Daimler died in Canstatt on 6 March 1900.

**DURANT, William C** *(1861-1947)*
William Crapo Durant was born at Boston, Massachusetts, on 8 December 1861, and by 1886 had set up a carriage-building business in Michigan. After taking over another firm he began to construct Buick cars, merging this

Walter P. Chrysler

operation with those of several other manufacturers to form the General Motors Co in 1908. Due to financial wheeler-dealing, he lost control in 1910 but established the Chevrolet Motor Co with ex-racing driver Louis Chevrolet.

By manipulating shares, Durant placed this operation in a position where it was able to take over the General Motors Co in 1915 to form the General Motors Corp, with Durant as President. Business expanded well but the post World War I sales slump forced him out again in 1920. Undeterred, he founded Durant Motors Inc, again taking over various smaller organizations to diversify operations but neither this nor later ventures were very successful. He died in New York City in 1947.

**FODEN, Edwin R** *(1870-1950)*
Edwin Richard Foden was born on 28 March 1870 and followed in his father's footsteps with a great interest in things mechanical. His father ran the Foden traction engine and threshing machine business in Sandbach, Cheshire, and young Edwin was soon advising him on points of design. One of these was to construct a 2-cylinder machine that was both easier to start and smoother-running, thus leading to many new orders.

Edwin Richard's father died in 1911 and he took over the reins of the firm. He was the first to use pneumatic tyres on a steam wagon and developed a number of very advanced designs but the authorities were anti-steam and he began to investigate diesel power at the end of the 1920s. His colleagues on the board were not interested and so, for both business and health reasons, he retired to Blackpool in 1930. He was not inactive, however, and pondered deeply on the possibilities of diesel. Then, in 1932, he began to construct his own prototype diesel lorry in a rented shed back at Sandbach with the assistance of

former Foden colleagues and son Dennis. Carrying the legend 'E R Foden & Son Diesel', the first ERF, as it was soon known, was well ahead of its time and a new factory was set up almost immediately with E R Foden as Managing Director.

Business built up rapidly and E R Foden remained an active participant until his death in 1950.

**FORD, Henry** *(1863-1947)*
Born the son of Irish immigrants in Wayne County, Michigan, on 30 July 1863, Henry Ford started his working life as a machinist's apprentice in Detroit at the age of 15. He soon moved back to the family farm and set up a small machine shop and sawmill, determined to make farm work a lot easier.

His persistence won him the post of Chief Engineer to the Edison Co, Detroit, which he held until 1899 when he set up the Detroit Automobile Co with some colleagues but left soon after to construct racing cars. This led to the formation of the Ford Motor Co in 1903 and the introduction of the immortal Model 'T' five years later. Ford soon earned himself a reputation for revolutionizing production techniques, his philosophy being to produce as many vehicles as possible and by so doing cut the price to the customer. By 1913 the Model 'T' was selling at just $500 and when discontinued in 1927 was replaced by the Model 'A'. A V8 petrol engine was developed in 1932 and gradually the company opened plants throughout the world, all employing mass-production techniques.

**LEVASSOR, Emile** *(1844-1897)*
Emile Levassor was a French inventor who, with René Panhard, took over a manufacturer of woodworking machinery in 1886 and began building his own version of the Daimler petrol engine for the French market on behalf

Gottlieb W. Daimler

of a Belgian entrepreneur. Unfortunately, this gentleman died suddenly so Levassor married his widow to whom the French Daimler rights had passed. He developed a revolutionary new car layout with horizontal engine ahead of the driver to provide good front wheel adhesion and a pinion-and-gearwheel transmission providing several alternative speeds. Such a layout was to become the norm for both cars and commercials of the immediate future.

Edwin R. Foden

**MORRIS, William R** *(1877-1963)*
Born in Worcestershire in October 1877, William Richard Morris was forced to give up his hopes of a medical career through his father's ill-health, beginning work at 15 by setting up a cycle repair shop behind his home. He also built cycles to order and raced them, later moving on to motorcycles and finally to cars. In 1903 he took a partner into the business but was soon bankrupt.

With a set of tools and a £50 debt, he established a small workshop at Cowley, Oxford, where he constructed the first Morris 'Oxford' 2-seater in 1913. Prosperity followed and he soon introduced the Morris 'Cowley', assembling this along Ford's mass-production lines. Morris Motors Ltd was founded in 1919 and in order to survive during 1920/1 all prices were slashed drastically. In 1923 his Morris Garages operation constructed the first MG and in the same year he formed Morris Commercial Cars Ltd to introduce mass-production techniques into the British truck industry.

In 1952 his vehicle-building activities were merged with those of the Austin Motor Co Ltd to form the British Motor Corp, which at the time was the third largest vehicle manufacturer in the world.

**OLDS, Ransom E** *(1864-1950)*
Claimed to be the first successful American vehicle manufacturer,

Ransom Eli Olds was born at Geneva, Ohio, in 1864 and as a young man quickly established a reputation as a first-rate inventor. His first 3hp curved-dash Olds appeared in the 1890s and in 1899 he established the Olds Motor Works, backed financially by Samuel L Smith, in Lansing, Michigan, to construct Oldsmobile cars on one of the world's first automotive assembly lines.

Unfortunately, a disagreement with Smith led to Old's resignation in 1904 after which he found the Reo Motor Car Co, the descendant of which was to become world-famous as a heavy truck producer.

**SELDEN, George B** *(1846-1922)*
Fully qualified as a lawyer, George Baldwin Selden, born 1846, was granted a patent for a revolutionary road engine in 1895 and sold the rights to this only on a royalty basis. For a while he had the entire American motor industry eating out of his hand but his monopoly was brought to an end by Henry Ford who stubbornly refused to pay. Selden took him to court and in a 1911 decision it was decreed that the Ford design was fundamentally different and royalties did not have to be paid.

**SIMMS, Frederick R** *(1863-1935)*
Frederick Richard Simms, born in 1863, was one of the great pioneers of the British motor industry, founding Simms & Co, consulting engineers, in 1890, which pioneered the use of low-tension

Frederick R. Simms

ignitions and the manufacture of motorboat engines and aerial cableways.

In 1901 Simms founded the Society of Motor Manufacturers & Traders, and was elected its first President. As well as building both cars and commercials in the early days, Simms's company concentrated on the manufacture of vehicle ignition systems and fuel-injection equipment during the 1930s but he resigned his position of Managing Director in 1935 and died nine years later.

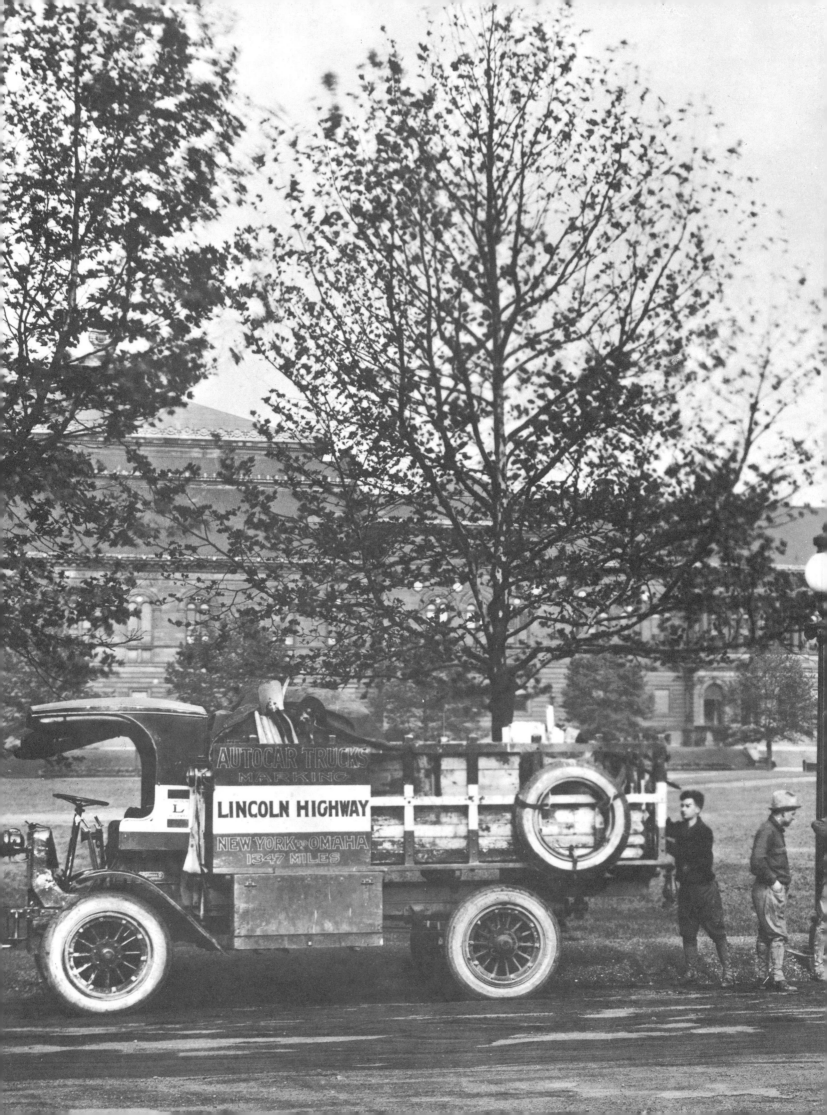